Under Blorenge Mountain

The Blaenavon Industrial Landscape is of 'outstanding universal value' and was inscribed as a World Heritage Site in November 2000 by the United Nations Educational Scientific and Cultural Organisation (UNESCO) under the World Heritage Convention.

> The area around Blaenavon bears an exceptional testimony to the pre-eminence of South Wales as the world's major producer of iron and coal in the nineteenth century. It is a remarkably complete example of a nineteenth-century landscape.
>
> *World Heritage Committee, November 2000*

Chris Morris has explored this exceptional landscape created in the formative years of the Industrial Revolution. With his artist's eye he reveals the well known monuments from new angles and in a new light. He also introduces us to corners we had not visited and to 'trivial' things we had passed by so often without truly appreciating.

Very importantly, he reminds us that this landscape was created by human endeavour. His lens captures some of the people of the area and shows that the strength of character that made Blaenavon great is still alive and well.

The Blaenavon Industrial Landscape has a wonderful story to tell and this lovely book interprets it for us in a very special way.

The Blaenavon Partnership has been pleased to assist Chris in publishing this book as it helps to realise our obligation to UNESCO to identify, protect, conserve, present and promote the World Heritage Site.

John Rodger MBE
Blaenavon Project Director

'Sometimes the difference between trivial and important doesn't seem to matter'

Dennis Potter

Under Blorenge Mountain

Blaenavon Industrial Landscape
World Heritage Site

Chris Morris

with an introduction by

Jan Morris

TANNER'S YARD PRESS

Acknowledgements

I would like to thank all those who helped in this project, especially:

Frank James, for introducing me to Blaenavon
John Rodger, for his sustained enthusiasm and support
Jan Morris, for generously contributing the introduction.

TYP gratefully acknowledges the assistance of the Blaenavon Partnership in the production of this book.
Images from Big Pit courtesy of National Museums and Galleries of Wales

First published 2003 by Tanners Yard Press
Church Road, Longhope, Gloucestershire GL17 0LA

Designed by Paul Manning
Printed and bound in Great Britain by The Charlesworth Group, Huddersfield, West Yorkshire

British Library Cataloguing in Publication Data
A catalogue record for this book is available from the British Library

ISBN 0 9542096 1 3

Iron land marker, Pwll-du

Introduction *by Jan Morris*

'Wales stood flamboyantly at the vortex of the world'

Castles and sea-beaches, watercolour valleys, mountains haunted by ancient legend – these are the classic allurements of Wales, which have drawn visitors to this country since the age of the picturesque. It is a fascinating paradox that one of the very first Welsh places listed by UNESCO as a World Heritage Site – a site, that is, of importance to all humanity – has no castle and no beaches, stands in bleak moorland country and was unknown to the fabulists of antiquity. It is the nineteenth-century iron-making town of Blaenavon, high among the headwaters of the southern

valleys, and one of the most truly iconic places in Wales.

Wales is a fringe country: on the fringe of a kingdom, on the fringe of a continent and usually on the fringe of universal history. It is a country of profound and subtle meanings, but most of them are elusive, and are lost to a stranger's eye in the transcendent beauty of the place.

There was one brief period, however, when Wales stood flamboyantly at the vortex of the world. The epochal Industrial Revolution of the eighteenth and nineteenth

centuries, which changed the planet for ever, was largely fuelled by the minerals embedded in the mountains of southern Wales, and for a few decades the little nation was one of the most exciting places on earth. Thousands of Welsh people flocked from the countryside to the newly industrialised areas. Thousands of outsiders arrived from England, from Europe, even from America. Social orders were disarranged, immemorial habits went topsy-turvy, vast fortunes were made, great shipping lines were founded and a new genre of literature, in Welsh and in English, commemorated the tough, grimed, hybrid and forceful civilisation of the industrial valleys – 'the valleys', as they have been generically known ever since.

It did not last, as we all know. The coalfields were presently exhausted, the furnaces were dampened, the ships sailed in other seas and people no longer thought of Wales in terms of *How Green Was My Valley*. But the almost volcanic eruption of Welsh energies that ushered humanity into a new age left a host of relics behind. That feisty industrial society of the valleys has not lost its tang; the radical fervour of the workforce is not exhausted; and all over the southern coastlands, valleys and mountains there remain, in one vast and fascinating memorial, a vast industrial detritus – pit-wheels and mine-shafts, canals and foundries and forges, the tramroads that were the forerunners of our railroads, mansions for the tycoons, cottages for the labourers.

At an emblematic apex of this great testimony to a people and a historic moment stands the subject of this book: the nineteenth-century industrial town of Blaenavon and its surrounding landscape, which is now internationally recognised as a grand symbol of all our heritages.

Blaenavon is a world away from the tradi-

tional glories of Wales, but it possesses a different sort of magnetism – the magnetism of an idea. In this remote place, not so very long ago, it was demonstrated to all the nations that man could live by the energies of science and technology, fuelled by the resources of the earth. This is what the Industrial Revolution was about, and Blaenavon exemplifies its power, its excitement and its human sacrifices.

The Blaenavon Industrial Landscape World Heritage Site comprises an area of some 33 square kilometres, with the town itself at the core of it. Most of its peers on UNESCO's World Heritage roster possess one totemic structure – a cathedral, a seminal bridge, a leaning tower, a Great Wall. The presiding image of Blaenavon is more diffuse or even abstract, and is constructed of iron, brick, coal-dust, human muscle and a terrific landscape to form a unique whole. It is this powerful but intangible presence that Chris Morris commemorates in these pages, through the shapes and forms and attitudes of its buildings, its countryside and its people. Blaenavon is where a great historical progress had its birth – or at least got a hefty shove into motion – and everywhere in its streets, as in these pages, are reminders of its historic meaning.

In a way the town itself, compact and separate at the head of its valley, is like a reminder of earlier, rural times. There is little in it older than the late eighteenth century, and its entire *raison d'être* was the extraction and processing of iron ore, coal and limestone, but to this day it is not unlike a country hill town in some much easier environment. Its presiding Anglican church stands graciously in its churchyard, its parallel main streets run rather quaintly down the hillside, its rows of workmen's cottages look pretty enough, the iron-master's mansion is

'That feisty industrial society of the valleys has not lost its tang'

like a squire's seat and the little Afon Lwyd river rushes sportingly by. It is true that half the things in that church, even to the font, are made of iron, that there are several very Welsh Nonconformist chapels and the most grandiose building in town is the flamboyant Workmen's Hall. Still, at first sight one would not guess how fierce and demanding were the origins of this tight and companionable little place.

It is when you walk beyond its hospitable streets (for its people are famously friendly) that the real impact of Blaenavon strikes you. On the very edge of town stand the original iron-works, founded in 1789 and the best-preserved such monument on earth, a jumble of hefty furnace buildings and kilns with the houses of the workers in the middle. Just across the river, in the district called Forgeside where iron is still treated, the scientist Sydney Gilchrist Thomas, in the 1870s, perfected the Bessemer process of refining steel, which was fatefully to transform the industrial power of all Europe. And when you leave the little town behind you, and emerge upon the high, windy moor above, then the meaning of the Blaenavon idea is laid before you with a vengeance. In the middle distance are the hills that stand above the idyllic valley of the Usk, and out of sight down below is a once-vital canal, now in leisurely retirement; but the foreground is dramatic wasteland.

The Industrial Revolution exploded, triumphed and swept away from Wales like a hurricane, and perhaps its most magnificent and terrible deposits surround Blaenavon. In the summer the landscape may be happily crowded with tourists, but for myself I prefer to contemplate it on a cold winter day. Then it is like a silent battlefield up there, the sort of place where military historians look around for trenches, fortifications or even rusted guns. Instead of weapons, though, here are the remains of that original industrial convulsion; huge coaltips and abandoned tramroads, lonely pubs where the miners used to drink, terraces of workers' houses, walls made of iron, quarries and tunnels, a slag-heap in monstrous silhouette, long-deserted hamlets and that once-teeming canal. A solitary train, perhaps, maintained for the holiday trade, crawls across the wide landscape: a solitary pitwheel stands high and lonely above the Big Pit, one of the earliest of the deep coalmines of Wales, now no more than a museum of the whole lost mining industry.

It is a marvellous scene, but bitter-sweet. What hard, harsh lives were led here, by generations of ironworkers and mining people! What brilliant minds were applied to the ideas of Blaenavon! And what a tumultuous, colourful, brutal, creative culture was fostered here! Now all is silent, all is but memorial, and the Welsh flag flies above the Big Pit, proud but tattered, frayed by the incessant winds of the high moorland.

The labouring armies of the Industrial Revolution have gone, but their descendants and their values remain, and it is only proper that Chris Morris's moving tribute to Blaenavon should end with images of some of the very last working miners of the place, twenty-first-century incarnations of old traditions – still extracting coal from the mountain above, undismayed and undeterred, it seems, by all the effects of history upon their people, their landscape and their truly allegorical town.

Blaenavon: Two Centuries of Change

In 1785 the head of the Afon Lwyd valley, between Coity Mountain to the west and Blorenge to the north east, was peaceful sheep country and, occasionally, noisy grouse moor. In tandem with this rural scene there had been a tradition of limestone quarrying and mining for iron ore, but on a tiny scale.

This all changed when three businessmen from the Midlands moved in with a big idea: to set up an ironworks. The timing was not accidental: coke was newly discovered as a smelting fuel, and steam power had arrived. The new fuel enabled the area's rich resources of iron ore, coal and limestone (together with fire clay, and sandstone as building material) to be efficiently harnessed on an unprecedented scale; the new power source meant that location was a choice, not dependent on a stream.

So confident were Hill, Hopkins and Pratt when they set up the Blaenavon Iron Company in 1787, leasing a huge tract of mountain from Lord Abergavenny, that they set about constructing not one but three furnaces. Over the next couple of decades the infrastructure broadened to provide a supply chain for the raw materials they needed, and delivery routes for the product; added value was provided by an early forge, sited further down the valley at Cwmavon, where pig iron could be re-cast or converted to wrought iron. This then went on down the valley to the Monmouthshire Canal, to Newport and the coast.

By 1817 a new forge was operating at Garn-ddyrys, high on the north-west shoulder of Blorenge. A complex of ponds and leats was created to supply it with water, and a tunnel through the mountain (the longest in the world at the time) made a tramroad connection with the ironworks. There was a symbiotic gain to be made in choosing this high, bleak and wild spot for the forge: the wagons carrying pig iron to it were able to make the return journey laden with limestone from the Pwll-du quarry (situated just below the tramroad route as it snaked round the head of Cwm Llanwenarth). From Garn-ddyrys the tramroad's level line was continued east from the forge, round the north edge of Blorenge, dropping in a series of inclines to the Brecknock and Abergavenny Canal at Llanfoist; this was a better link to the outside world, with cheaper tariffs for iron. Later the Pwll-du tunnel was supplemented by an up-and-over route – the Dyne-Steel double incline.

By the mid-nineteenth century a modernisation programme was put in hand; new furnaces and a forge were built together in premises across the Afon Lwyd valley, the area becoming known as Forgeside. The Garn-ddyrys forge was closed by 1860, and the railway, now reaching up the valley from Pontypool, spelled the demise of canal transport.

Coal mining developed in the valleys to supply the furnaces, but in the end it overtook iron as the prime industry. Iron and steel began to move to the coast, and by 1900 coal was king. Big Pit, one of many collieries around Blaenavon, was the last to close (though a drift mine in the valley is still in production). Forgeside lives on too, with a modern engineering firm flourishing in the revamped premises.

As for the town, it endures, with a new sense of pride and optimism engendered by its World Heritage Site status. The churches

**Sketch map of Blaenavon
and surrounding area,
showing key locations
illustrated in this book**

The best large-scale map
of the area is OS OL13
(Brecon Beacons).

Not all sites enjoy open
access. Please respect
private property.

*Map references to less obvious
sites:*

Aaron Brute's Bridge	248088
Bessemer Wall	250097
Blaenavon Co. Marker	244117
Blaentillery No. 2 Mine	234092
Brake Engine	242099
Capel Newydd	269076
Carreg-Maen-Taro	238113
Coity Quarry	232093
Dyne Steel (summit)	241111
Govilon Warehouse	269137
Hill's Chimney	239102
Hill's Tramroad/B4246	260121
Llanfoist Incline (head)	277127
Lord Abergavenny	
Marker	250117
Pwll-du Quarry	252115
Pwll-du Tunnel	
(N. portal)	244117
Wildon Forge	259134

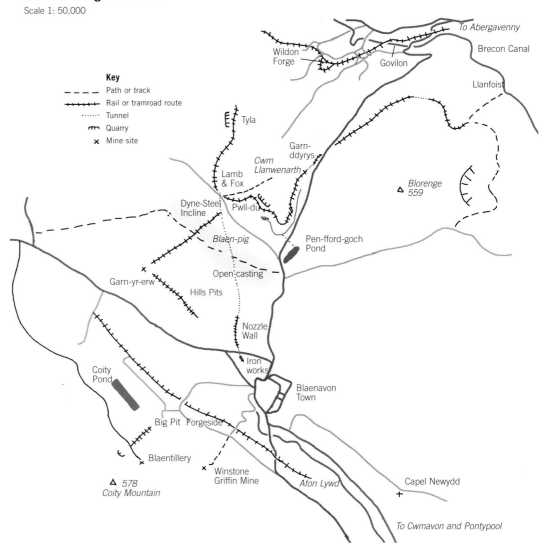

Under Blorenge Mountain

Scale 1: 50,000

Key
- – – – Path or track
- +++ Rail or tramroad route
- .... Tunnel
- Quarry
- ✕ Mine site

and myriad chapels fit snugly amidst the terraced housing, with the Workmen's Hall and Institute still an imposing presence in the centre.

While the two big sites, Big Pit and the Ironworks, might seem to dominate Blaenavon's industrial legacy, the landscape around the town is rich in interest. The scars of the mining itself, ranging in scale from pre-industrial pits to the great gashes left by the open-casting of the 1950s, are laced with the remnants of the tramroads, the ponds and leats, all intermingled with the ubiquitous sheep, the original inhabitants, the industrial survivors.

9

The Ironworks

This is where the Blaenavon story really starts. Industrial, urban and social development all followed the setting up of the North Street furnaces in 1787.

Raw materials were loaded at the top level; wagonloads of pig-iron, cast at the bottom level, were raised back up to the tramroad in the water balance lift tower *(facing page)*.

International interest can be judged by the American Society of Metals plaque *(right)* and the visit of a German film crew, lighting up the casting sheds for a UNESCO documentary *(below)*.

BLAENAVON IRON WORKS HAS BEEN DESIGNATED AN HISTORICAL LANDMARK BY AMERICAN SOCIETY FOR METALS

THE SITE OF THE BIRTHPLACE OF THE BASIC STEEL PROCESS DEVELOPED BY SYDNEY GILCHRIST THOMAS IN 1878. THIS PROCESS TRANSFORMED STEELMAKING THROUGHOUT THE WORLD BY ALLOWING THE ABUNDANT HIGH PHOSPHOROUS ORES TO BE EXPLOITED.

1985

The Ironworks – furnaces

In a view towards the casting house, light streams down No. 3 furnace (*right*).

The top of No. 4 furnace (*above*), shows how the facing stone has been stripped away, used to build St James Church (*page 40*).

The Ironworks – casting

The fire-bricks revealed through their eroded black iron casing are lining a 'cupola' furnace (*right*), used to cast small items; more complex castings, such as those used in Aaron Brute's Bridge (*above*), an important structure of 1812, were probably made on another site.

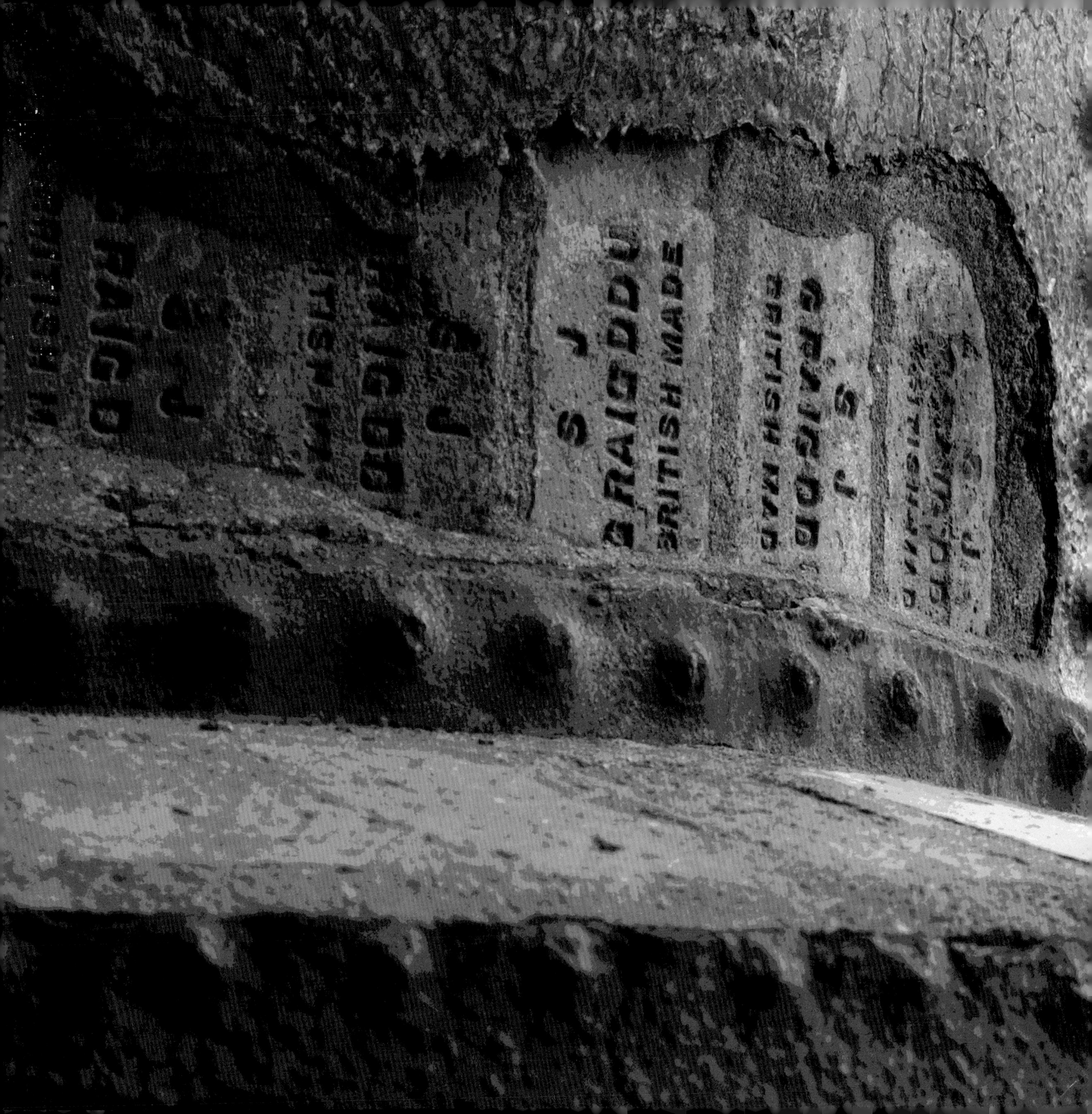
S J
CRAIGDDU
BRITISH MADE

Cwmavon

The first forge in the valley is now a peaceful pony paddock. The dam in the Afon Lwyd controlled the water supply; above the site stand the workers' cottages, Forge Row, listed and restored, and the forge manager's residence, Cwmavon House.

Bill Price, ex-Big Pit miner, and his wife Rose live in Forge House, in the middle of the site. Soon after they moved there, in 1976, a party of academics came to view the still extensive evidence of the forge. 'We didn't want our field to be public,' said Rose. 'I called in my friend Phil with his digger and we flattened it.'

Garn-ddyrys

There is little left of this early forge, set high on Blorenge. The outstanding feature is the pile of slag; below this are several enigmatic ruins with vaulting and underground entrances.

High on the site are two level walled areas which were ponds, fed by leats *(page 20)*; the forge itself was between the slag and the ponds.

Hill's Tramroad *(page 24)* passed through the site, partly in a tunnel – possibly to save working space.

Pen-fford-goch Pond

This pond, high on the saddle between Blorenge and its western ridge (known locally as Blaen-pig), was built as a reservoir. Water, controlled by sluice, dropped into the head of Cwm Llanwenarth, then ran in 'contour leats' almost level along the slope to supply Garn-ddyrys forge.

Pwll-du

The iron handrail (*facing page*) and Lord Abergavenny's land marker (*below*) can be seen on the Gothens path, leading down to Cwm Llanwenarth.

Hill's Tramroad (*page 22*) runs level to the top of Pwll-du quarry; as at the Ironworks, a water balance lift was employed, to raise limestone to the tramroad's level: the top of its shaft is still visible *(left)*. Debris of ruined buildings remain on the quarry floor (*below left*).

Hill's Tramroad

The tramroad was the vital link in utilising the Garn-ddyrys site. Existing coal workings were extended to create the Pwll-du tunnel, linking the Ironworks with the quarries and the forge.

The tunnel's southern portal is buried by open-casting, but at the north end one of two exits survive (*below*) just west of the Lamb and Flag pub. That branch led west to Tyla Quarry; another, the portal buried, turned east towards Garn-ddyrys, connecting en route with Pwll-du Quarry.

To the east of Garn-ddyrys, the tramroad route continued level along the northern flank of Blorenge. Some sections still reveal the stones with their rail fixing holes. After a short tunnel *(below)* the route dropped down inclines to the Brecknock and Abergavenny Canal wharf at Llanfoist.

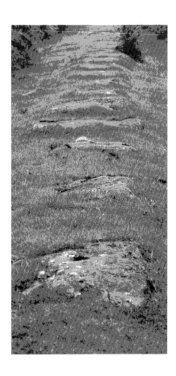

Llanfoist

The wharf and warehouse, and the house of the 'wharfinger', are intact at what today is a thriving holiday boat yard. The canal, now named the Monmouthshire & Brecon, is still being restored to the east.

The recreation with a horse-drawn barge (*facing page*) was for a UNESCO documentary film (*page 10*).

Govilon

Frank Cooke's smallholding includes land under both railway and tramroad viaducts, on the site of Wildon Forge.

The metal plate of a weighbridge (*facing page*) lies on part of what was the canal wharf; the Blaenavon Company's warehouse (its loading bracket, *below left*) can be seen under the bridge.

The bridge may have originally been part of the tramroad – the route down the mountain is uncertain – so pre-dates the notice stipulating axle loads.

Dyne-Steel Incline

When traffic got too busy through the tramroad tunnel, a double incline was built to augment it. It crossed the ridge from above Garn-yr-erw in the south to Pwll-du in the north, rejoining the old tramroad at the tunnel exit (*page 24*) by the Lamb and Fox pub. Wagons going north were balanced by limestone from the quarries heading in to the Ironworks.

At the summit the incline has been broken by open-casting, and industrial remnants tend to be from that period. Abandoned cars may be an unwelcome sight but do provide a certain irony, their rusting steel shells disintegrating into the land scarred from earlier iron-ore extraction.

Half a mile west along the ridge an ancient stone, Carreg-Maen-Taro, proclaims 'B' for Brecon on the county line.

Forgeside

In the mid-nineteenth century the Blaenavon Company expanded across the valley to new premises, with furnaces and forge on one site; a new community settled beside it, the area becoming known as Forgeside.

Zion Baptist Chapel *(below right)* is set amongst the terraces; the other doorway is to the nearby 'Electric House', an early-twentieth-century sub-station.

A modern engineering firm, Doncasters *(facing page)*, today occupies the old industrial site; in the yard Coity House *(right)* stands sadly derelict (although listed); in the factory itself an old press stands for continuity, working parts for today's jet engines.

The Town

Before the town took shape housing was built adjacent to the workplace; Stack Square at the Ironworks *(above)* is an example. This policy often led to isolated terraces scattered on the open land; many have been demolished (for example, at Pwll-du and Garn-ddyrys), but others, as at Forgeside, viewed beyond the High Street *(right)* and at Garn-yr-erw *(page 46)* can still be seen.

St Peter's Church, 1805

Central to the town's development, paid for by the ironmasters, St Peter's has a cast-iron font, iron columns and capitals and iron window-frames.

In the graveyard Danny Watkins, church treasurer, inspects one of several casket tombs with iron covers.

Workmen's Hall and Institute

Including the almost inevitable iron columns and capitals, this building is a monument to the era of workers' self-improvement. Opened in 1895, it was paid for by subscription from Union funds. It is said that the kitty was augmented as Big Pit miners, sneaking off their shift early by the River Gate level, were levied a fine by a Union man waiting at the exit.

The clock tower is the town's war memorial.

Demolition and Devotion

An iron cross marks the site of Capel Newydd, an outlying chapel of Llanover, pre-dating Blaenavon parish.

St James church, now a carpenter's workshop, was built with stone stripped off the furnaces at the old Ironworks (*page 12*).

Bethlehem Chapel, 1840, named as it first opened on Christmas Eve, has iron supports to the front balustrading; Mrs Morris, secretary, (left in the group) leads the lunchtime 'sisterhood' prayer meetings.

Cafe Culture

That Blaenavon can prosper under the mantle of its new World Heritage status is confirmed by the cafés, estate agent's and antique shops gracing its steep grey streets. The optimism in Broad Street is exemplified by Mr and Mrs Lewis and their staff (*facing page*).

The cafés date from the late nineteenth century when immigrants arrived from southern Italy. 'Bracchi houses' (a name possibly derived from the Breccia marble used for the counters) appeared in every high street. The Belli family run no fewer than three in Blaenavon.

With a nod to this tradition, Liptons (*right*) has complemented the ceramic tiles of the converted grocery shop with an espresso machine from Parma, and marble imported all the way from an old 'Bracchi house' in Abertillery.

Hill's Pits

Many coal and iron mines were sited along the valley side to the west of the Ironworks, linked by Hill's Tramroad. The best remnants are the chimney and ruined building at Hill's Pits.

What looks like a man-trap (*facing page*) is a 'brake-engine', a device for slowing loaded trams descending an incline. The section of field wall (*below left*) is made from 'nozzles' of fire-brick, used for blasting hot air through the floor of a bessemer converter.

Garn-yr-erw

This is an area strewn with tips, frequented only by sheep and illegal bikers.

The abandoned pump (*below*) underlines the importance of water as a resource, and the threat it posed to underground working.

Open Casting

To the north-west of the town, small-scale tips give way to the larger-scale remains of open casting, reaching up to the summit ridge of Blaen-pig *(previous page)*.

Brian Lewis *(facing page)* has lived most of his life high on the mountain at the Lamb and Fox; he is a conservationist, planting trees to create a shelter belt around the pub.

While sympathetic to the Heritage Site, he emphasises that his respect is for the manual effort involved: 'When you look at the old workings, you think of the men who shaped this land by the shovelful.' In his view the hundreds of acres of open casting dug and dumped by bulldozer do not merit the same concern and should be landscaped.

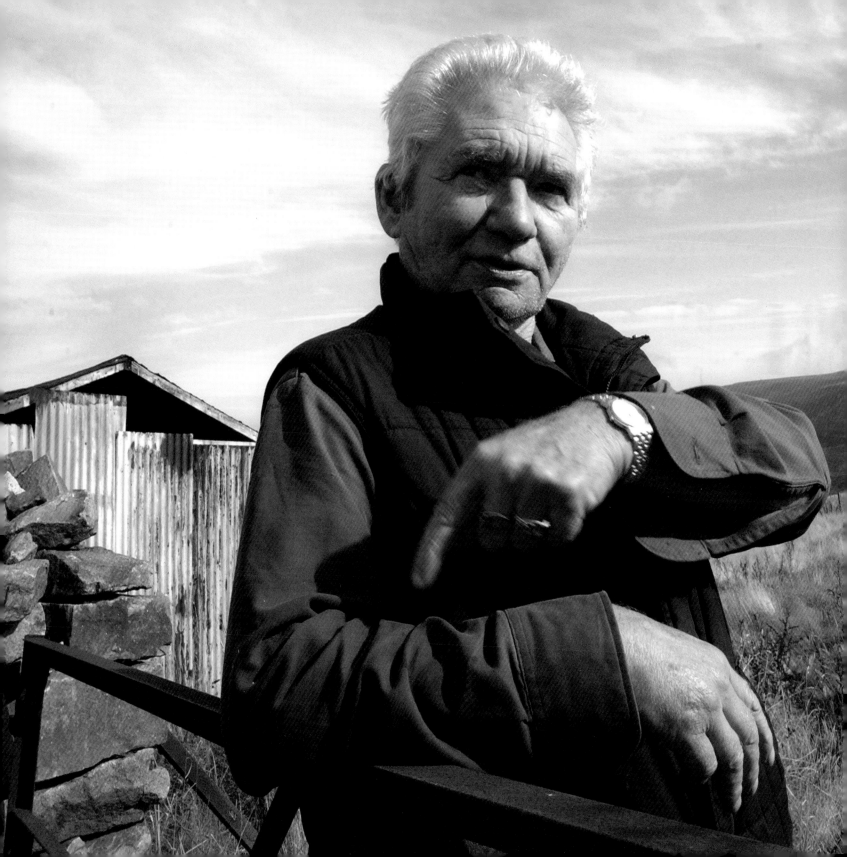

Big Pit

Big Pit was the last of Blaenavon's deep collieries to close, shutting down operations in 1980.

Today it lives on as the hugely popular National Mining Museum of Wales.

Big Pit — going under

A main attraction is the underground tour, conducted by ex-miners including John Tovey *(above)* and Colin Dunn *(below)*. At the pit top, Graham Gratton, chief electrical engineer, stands by the lift cage *(right)*.

Big Pit – Bath House

The bath house contains the locker room *(previous page)*, the shower rooms *(facing page)* and boilers.

The construction of pithead baths benefited the women in the community as much as the men: hours of heating up water for the tin bath in the kitchen became a thing of the past.

The 1930s 'International Style' architecture *(right)* is being restored.

Big Pit – overground

One of the overground attractions: the blacksmith's shop where Len Howell has been making sparks for half a lifetime

The Railway

In the middle of the nineteenth century the railway from Newport and Pontypool came up the valley to Blaenavon; coupled with the new development at Forgeside, this spelled the demise of tramroad and canal transport.

A short stretch of railway adjacent to Big Pit remains open, run by local enthusiasts.

On Coity Mountain

High on the mountain is a quarry that provided sandstone for Big Pit's development; the cuttings and bank of the incline that led down the mountainside are still visible *(left)*.

To the west is Coity pond, Big Pit's water supply.

Winstone/Griffin Mine

A short way up the mountain above Forgeside, this drift mine, though clearly abandoned, displays all the paraphernalia of a working colliery.

The lowest level has a screening wall and coal shutes; above that is the main working area, connected by an enclosed stairway to a higher terrace with a second mine entrance.

Blaentillery No. 2 Colliery

This drift mine, still in production, employs fifteen men. Hidden from the valley by a landscaped bank, it is in fact directly above Big Pit.

Blaentillery –
coming off the shift

Des Williams *(above)*,
John Perrot *(right)*,
Alan Williams and Mark
Griffiths *(facing page)*

Also by Chris Morris

Work in the Woods, Dean's Industrial Heritage (Tanners Yard Press), a visual celebration of the Forest of Dean's industrial sites

Further Reading

Wales, Jan Morris (Penguin) – a definitive history

Exploring Blaenavon Industrial Landscape, Chris Barber (Blorenge Books), a richly illustrated guidebook

Photographic Note

Photography is a very broad-based discipline, allowing for a multiplicity of approaches and aspirations. Hence I have always been a little shy of any attempt to define 'photographic quality', quoted as it always is in the singular.

 I have used alternative techniques in my work for many years and regard digital equipment (Nikon 950 and D1X and Photoshop) as a natural progression.

At Blaenavon I have attempted to balance my graphic, sometimes semi-abstract, style (which provides the subject-matter with the drama it deserves), with the need to provide enough information to tell the story.

C.M.